Title page woodcut by Hans
Baldung Grien from Johannes
Grüninger's 1515 edition of
Eulenspiegel's adventures.

The Garland Library
of Medieval Literature

General Editors
James J. Wilhelm, Rutgers University
Lowry Nelson, Jr., Yale University

Literary Advisors
Ingeborg Glier, Yale University
William W. Kibler, University of Texas
Norris J. Lacy, Washington University
Giuseppe Mazzotta, Yale University
Fred C. Robinson, Yale University
Aldo Scaglione, University of North Carolina

Art Advisor
Elizabeth Parker McLachlan, Rutgers University

Music Advisor
Hendrik van der Werf, Eastman School of Music

TILL EULENSPIEGEL
His Adventures

translated,
with introduction
and notes, by

Paul Oppenheimer

Volume 74
Series B
GARLAND LIBRARY OF MEDIEVAL LITERATURE

Garland Publishing, Inc.
New York & London
1991

Library of Congress Cataloging-in-Publication Data

Eulenspiegel (Satire). English
    Till Eulenspiegel : his adventures / translated by Paul
Oppenheimer.
        p.   cm. — (Garland library of medieval literature ; v.
74. Series B)
    Translation of: Eulenspiegel.
    Includes bibliographical references.
    ISBN 0–8240–5754–6 (alk. paper)
    1. Oppenheimer, Paul. II. Title. III. Series: Garland library of
medieval literature ; v. 74.
PT941.E8E5   1991
833'.3—dc20   90–26368
                                                                     CIP

Printed on acid-free, 250-year-life paper
Manufactured in the United States of America

To Julie (ancora) and Ben too

Preface of the General Editors

The Garland Library of Medieval Literature was established to make available to the general reader modern translations of texts in editions that conform to the highest academic standards. All of the translations are originals, and were created especially for this series. The translations attempt to render the foreign works in a natural idiom that remains faithful to the originals.

The Library is divided into two sections: Series A, texts and translations; and Series B, translations alone. Those volumes containing texts have been prepared after consultation of the major previous editions and manuscripts. The aim in the edition has been to offer a reliable text with a minimum of editorial intervention. Significant variants accompany the original, and important problems are discussed in the Textual Notes. Volumes without texts contain translations based on the most scholarly texts available, which have been updated in terms of recent scholarship.

Most volumes contain Introductions with the following features: (1) a biography of the author or a discussion of the problem of authorship, with any pertinent historical or legendary information; (2) an objective discussion of the literary style of the original, emphasizing any individual features; (3) a consideration of sources for the work and its influence; and (4) a statement of the editorial policy for each edition and translation. There is also a Select Bibliography, which emphasizes recent criticism on the works. Critical writings are often accompanied by brief descriptions of their importance. Selective glossaries, indices, and footnotes are included where appropriate.

The Library covers a broad range of linguistic areas, including all of the major European languages. All of the important literary forms and genres are considered, sometimes in anthologies or selections.

The General Editors hope that these volumes will bring the general reader a closer awareness of a richly diversified area that has for too long been closed to everyone except those with precise academic training, an area that is well worth study and reflection.

James J. Wilhelm
Rutgers University

Lowry Nelson, Jr.
Yale University

TRANSLATOR'S PREFACE

This is in most important respects a new book and not simply a new edition of my translation of Till Eulenspiegel's adventures published in 1972. The translation has been extensively revised, the notes on the tales extended in what I hope will prove to be ways helpful to those interested in late medieval and Renaissance culture, and the Introduction much altered to take account of recent scholarship. If I have retained the theory of assertional language (under Artistic Achievement in the Introduction), I have done so in the trust that it holds as much validity today as it did when it was first conceived by a twenty-eight-year-old apprentice scholar.

I am deeply grateful to many people for many sorts of help: to my editor, Lowry Nelson Jr., who has offered numerous valuable suggestions for improving the manuscript; to James J. Wilhelm, for encouragement, important advice, and assistance; to Paula Ladenburg, my editor at Garland Publishing; to Dean Paul Sherwin of the Humanities Division of the City College of New York, for making his office with its facilities available to me; to Laryssa Barboza; and to Maria Correa, who has worked tirelessly to make this a better-appearing book. I am indebted as well to the staffs of The British Library, The New York Public Library, and The Library of the City College of New York for cooperation and assistance; and to Princeton University Library, from whose copy of the Schröder facsimile of the Grüninger edition of 1515 the woodcuts for this edition were reproduced. I also wish to acknowledge yet again the major corrections offered on very early versions of this book by the late W.T.H. Jackson, and by Howard Schless, both of Columbia University. The wealth of contributions from other scholars is, I trust, fully acknowledged in the text and bibliography. I am, finally, most grateful to Andras Hamori and Francesca Simpson Pedler, whose friendship and constant stream of good suggestions have enabled me to make this a better book than it otherwise would have been.

New York   P.O.
November 1990

CONTENTS